THE WHITE POEM

THE WHITE POEM

by

with photographs by

JAY RAMSAY

CAROLE BRUCE

Rivelin Grapheme & Five Seasons
1988

Photographs reproduced by the duotone process.
Printed by Adrian Lack at The Senecio Press Ltd,
Charlbury, Oxford. Text set in 14pt Sabon by
Patrick Roe at Glevum Graphics, Gloucester.
Designed and produced by Five Seasons Press,
Madley, Hereford—who publish THE WHITE POEM
in conjunction with Rivelin Grapheme Press,
The Annexe, Kennet House, 19 High Street,
Hungerford, Berkshire, RG17 0NL.

ISBN 0 947612 30 0 (paper)
        0 947612 29 7 (cloth)

for
our mothers
our fathers
and the earth herself

'But that of which the observer is really speaking is altogether invisible, and he is perfectly aware that the light or colour picture which he gives has no more to do with what he actually perceives than, for instance, the writing in which a fact is communicated has to do with the fact itself'

Rudolf Steiner

'You are spirits with a body, not bodies with a spirit—you always were and you always will be'

Silver Birch

'All that is visible must grow beyond itself, extend into the realm of the invisible'

I Ching tr. Richard Wilhelm

1

Invisible world.

I have come to the edge of you.

Standing here, in my body, at ease, as if on air
Breathing in silence . . .

I have learnt to stand still.

Now the sea mist rising
                              a thin stream of cloud
Up the sheer
                    falling away
                                        dark stone cliff face,
On the edge of where
                              the grass ends
                                                  & the air begins.

I dreamt of walking along a line
I was naked in the dream
I was as I am

And to the left of my spine, my back
And one moving thigh calf and heel,
The half of him that was visible

Walking towards a sun
Along the length of a low broken boundary wall:

And then a little later on in inside time
I was awake sitting up on this jutting-out rock
It was cold and I was talking to you on tape,
I was opening as far as I could into the place

That is slow and which only the body knows—
This body of air
                        this space from which words
Occur and rise
                        to the mouth
                                          this sea of air
This body swims
                        in its deepest speech into
This invisible space
                        between the words
                                          white space

Sky space

        sky page

                the real page

And it began as a disc of green oscillating light
I watched it come out between my eyes—
I watched it coming out of my mind—the low tide
Sand and distant twilight headland behind it,

And it became the horizon, and expanded
And was green and then yellow and then white
Light being given back, into me, from it

As it gently grew huge and whitened
And was a white hole a white sun and in the sun
A colossal figure was standing, the male
Or female body partly hooded in a loose cloak
And the face serenely in profile looking away to one side—
Irradiating light between my eyes,

And my eyes were open.

                . . .

I call this the edge of the world,
We are alone here
              surrounded here
                            as if on a mountain;

The path trailing off to the car park
And the cluster of hamlet houses
Their lead roofs and whitewashed walls—
The way you can look sometimes at something
Until it begins to disappear, its
Apparent solidity become light, the face
Of someone become featureless
                        presence
                              become space
The foreground fading
                 the sea rocks
                       blending in mist;

As you kneel and peer down to where a group of gulls
Hover round one of the rocks split by swirling froth,
And past the tangled barbed wire fence
With its tufts of sheep's wool
                                        the cliff falling
Among scraps
                of abandoned material—

And out,
Over the edge
                    watching a gull
                                        flying out, apart
the grey mist white of it
                                        beat by slow soundless beat
of its beak
                    eye
                        and wings

becoming invisible.

2

Now enter this whiteness, where your steps are leading you
Back into that churchyard with its newly laid grave,
And the shock of suddenly all those bright twilit flowers
Taking your breath back—

                    and held it, bending down
Close where the rain

                had smudged & blurred the handwriting

scrawled messages of farewell
to a dead man's soul
gone into the mist

gone into the mind, this human fleshed thing
become like a body of decaying words

gone out of the body into the mind,
as the thought the half-glimpsed image of it comes through

where we go through

from this charged place of him under the dug earth
on this edge where only the one sense can penetrate

to him that was him laid down here,
and him nowhere here at all, nothing at all

And as the waves roll in, coming in, out of the mist
Stirring in their white windblown crests

you come to the point
the point in my mind I reach
and ceaselessly fall back from

into the waves,
                    the waves,
                                the waves.

3

Something invisible in you brought you there
You came back, shaken, your tears blown away by the air
And told me. You turned from a trickling spring, saw it:
A great black cormorant splayed flat, its wings outstretched.
And then a gannet a few yards further on

And then a sheep with its belly ripped open
And then — your camera: jammed. And something unnameable
In you it took the whole week to start working through;
This intuitive fact of our being what happens
It is not fixed, nor is it random

But in that fluid space between, there, wherever you are
The place is you as strangely as you tell me your dream;
And that dead beach that haunted you was a mirror
Of all that it brought up in you, on the threshold

Of that dead life you died in.

4

Dead body of house behind rusting iron farm gate
Open to the wind and to everything

An empty bottle drinking in water from the stream
Reflecting the weeds like trees in the undertow

And the rafters piled among plaster, and broken
Slates; and past a fallen roof-section, the outhouses

Become blended totally with the brambles, ivy & nettles.
Stairs you could walk up into the sky on—

And the sky, the thin blue endless abyss of it
Curving from the top of my head where I'm standing

And then inside the open walls, four square spaces
Through the empty front door framing
Under the contact sheet magnifier

your hidden face
only you can enter
and in the shadow
                        of what the earth is turning & turning
through
            the shadow-whole of what you
have passed through—
                                intact
ghost of you
                standing behind you

in your being that is living here,
this human ghost that is in shadow here
this valley of shadow you & I
are going through

this memory-landscape
                    dreamscape
                                    dream of life

threading out, as we talk
inside and out
of its invisible
                    lens-like
                                    beyond sense centre

that is light,
the image exposed
in fluent light
                    moving
                                    behind each image

wind and wave sway
and mood of face
tone of voice
                    coded, visibly, approximately

in process
of becoming the evolving
point of itself
                    in the mind's eye
                                    the source

at flashpoint
trigger point and each line
of this as we are together traced

                                  along the length
of its opened-out labyrinth

                            of outside & inside
and at their · of intersection

                              and across a threshold

that is blank white space

        between us

                each line of this

filling and then fading

        each word of it you speak

on this air as it warms

        in its invisible ink white

and then vanishes,
is revised, is replaced
—whited out, retyped—

        begun again

            in the mind's eye

the body's source

      at the deep interior

                                      the earth
meditates & your mind mediates—

on this side of physical life,
as the road bends round and the stout open fence
borders the white sun's sea

the bare sailless mast of a moored yacht
heavy length of anchor chain on harbour stone
and the body deliberately treading the ground
and a solitary white car accelerating out of the mist;

and my body lying
                        down on the pebbles, letting
the sea sound
                        cover me and the thought happen
thinking in white
                        textures of white . . .
fallen feathers
                        white sheets and the lines on this
cuttlefish, and this hand
                        and the blind touch
of a magnolia petal
                        felt between finger-and-thumb
with the eyes closed,
walking, in step with each step
in my skin
                        and the skin of you I touch

through the sound of running water, and behind you
as the firelight mounts
                                                in a time
                        turned inside out
                into space

5

World visible and invisible
Become thought, visibly—
And in my body, my body you can see
And in my voice, and that which speaks
This voice

as the print rises
                    rubbed under your fingertips
up on the floating
                    surface of the paper

And if you took away the space
From the atoms within me
I would become what I am behind this image
I would become that vanishing

shadow-on-the-gravel,
                    focussed in this illusion
of spaced particles
                    that shape him as human.

Midnight lunar aureole of light,
Crouching by the window breathing the night's cool depth
And over the surface of my skin
Beginning to feel

that closening
                    tuned sense that these hands
                                                    touch
around your head
                    white figure, white presence

Distilled in skin, moonlit, bathing in it
Spoken in this clearness of your whispering voice
The sound of you in a being that is beyond ghost,
Come through in its full subtle strength

slow heartbeat tremor
                                the stillness vibrating
                                                        embodied
on the edge of each slow white second's ending

In a square of white developed space,
Edge where this visible world of what we are
Enters into its energy
                            the hand's slow moving
soundless sound
                    of white on white, the traced letters illegibly
beyond me
                as it shapes & images each inch of this paraphrase

On the untouched pages
Of a book—a blank white book
Cover and each page I am turning—the whole thing

as I am standing in this
                              spirit body
                                        Self that is here

From the body's depth, dreamt, drawn
Unfolding from its elemental image, earth-
Born bound and connected

to this air body of voice and speech
                                        that is *I am*
                                                  sunk
in the shadow light where each life
                                        is being written

And deep in the closening distance where you have come
To stand beyond yourself in this moment of your mind here

gone through the body into the mind
coming back to flood the body with light

This is the sacrifice
Crossing the threshold now beyond all holding back

surrendered
            filled
                    as with you—

And the whole of it brought back into this mirage
Of our dehumanized suffering nothingness
Plane of which we are the makers and the reflections
Death of what we are dying through

                                into this whiteness
of spirit self

              filtering, worked

                        consciously & complex

From within what we are invisibly journeying towards
Beyond this shrunken horizon of ourselves,

from this co-

              nnection, source of our

                        extension continuing
as indelibly as we are continued—

Now it comes through as the sun fades to twilight

And outside, the silverlit leaf rustling wind

And in the silence where I have gone beyond him to meet you.

April–July 1985
Pembrokeshire & London

acknowledgements

The quote from Rudolf Steiner is from *On The Threshold Of The Spiritual World* (Steiner Press); Silver Birch, the spirit guide, quoted by Nadia Fowler in *Tom Pilgrim: the autobiography of a spiritual healer* (Sphere Books); and the *I Ching* (hexagram: The Cauldron), translated by Richard Wilhelm (Routledge and Kegan Paul).

Quotations from the poem, in the context of a joint article ('Pembrokeshire: Working Notes For *The White Poem*') first appeared in *The Green Book*, along with four of the photographs.

The photographs were first exhibited at the National Poetry Centre Gallery (September–October 1986) under the title *Edge Of Light*, organised by Pamela Clunies-Ross. Both earlier, and more recent pictures (taken in Provence and Derbyshire) appear in *Psycho-synthesis Forum*, following a personal testimony.

Our deep and heartfelt thanks to those who gave their love and support to this project, without which this book could not have been published: Diana and John Storey (Gerah Industries, Sydney, Australia), Joan and Roger Evans (the London Institute of Psychosynthesis), Sir George Trevelyan, Lizzie Spring, Inge Killick, Dinah Molloy, Patricia Villiers-Stuart, Jane Shilling, Katy Bruce, Alan Pickett and Jackie Wray.

Finally to Glenn Storhaug, our publisher and friend, for his design and sensitivity; to Adrian Lack for his care over the photographs; and to Snowdon Barnett for his faith in it—

C. B. and J. R.